POWER TOOLS
Move Over Machiavelli

By
Gaylen K. Bunker

BusinessAllStars, Salt Lake City, Utah 84109

Table of Contents

Tragedy in Paradise   1

Niccollo' Machiavelli   7

Who Are the Powerful?   14

Control the Message   18

Own the Market   28

Unregulated is Best   39

Shift the Risk   48

Influence the Influential   59

No Disclosure   69

A Case Study   76

Summary   80

Reactions to the COUSIN Theory   83

Terms   85

Acknowledgements

I have been developing the concepts for this book over an extended period of time. It has been the result of observations about the real world as contrasted with the textbook principles that I have taught at the MBA and undergraduate level.

There is always pressure to publish and present papers at conferences. At a casual meeting with another colleague, Dr. Ron Mano, PhD we were discussing possible avenues for publication. I mentioned that I had an idea and showed him my COUSIN theory. He became quite excited and suggested that I pursue it.

I prepared a first draft of this document and had him review it. He was very encouraging and so we presented my paper at a couple of conferences. The reception we received was very interesting. He has continued to encourage me to develop this idea and I want to thank him for his encouragement and support.

Gaylen K. Bunker

Tragedy in Paradise

It was a beautiful moon lit evening in Tonga, a tropical paradise and isolated kingdom 6,000 miles from California and 2,000 from Australia. In the little village of Ngele'ia, a young attractive Peace Corps volunteer, Deb Gardner, had completed another exhausting day helping the locals and was getting ready for bed. It was about 9:45 pm and she slipped out of her clothes and into a white nightdress.

Suddenly, the door burst open and standing there was a fellow volunteer, Dennis Priven. In his hand he held a metal pipe which he raised as he rushed at her. The frenzied maniac hit her with the pipe and then pulling a six-inch diving knife from his belt, he began to stab her over and over again. Twenty-two times the blade of the knife found its way into her body.

Clinging to life she began to scream and scream. He grabbed her and began pulling her to the door. The screaming alerted a nearby Tongan, To'a Pasa.

"I heard a scream. I know there's something happening in there," says To'a Pasa, who was just 15 at the time. He came running from his house across the road. "I was very scared. I was thinking to myself, 'There is someone there inside trying to rape her."

To'a Pasa recognized Priven dragging Garden through the front door in the full moon light. When Priven saw To'a Pasa he dropped Garden, went to his bicycle and pedaled off into the night. To'a Pasa summoned help immediately and Garden was transported to the hospital. On the way she was asked who had done it and she replied: Dennis Priven. Efforts were unsuccessful at the hospital to save her and she died that night.

Back at Gardner's cottage investigators found Priven's backpack, bloody six-inch diving-knife, one of his flip-flops, his glasses, a syringe, and a bottle of cyanide. The eye witness and evidence appeared to be conclusive, but what should have been a very simple case turned into a well-crafted cover-up by Peace corp officials.

Days before the incident there were signs that Priven was a potential problem. He was a very strange individual and seemed to have an obsession for Gardner. He was stalking her and making her life very uncomfortable. She became so fearful that she requested a transfer just to get away from him. "But the director of the office, a 47-year-old ex-model and political appointee named Mary George, did nothing."[1]

Following the murder that night everyone went looking for Priven, but it wasn't until the next morning that he turned himself in. Mary George instantly realized this was a major crisis for the Peace Corps and began the process of trying to control the message. In her first telex to Washington she

---

[1] http://www.cbsnews.com/stories/2005/06/15/48hours/main
702039_page2.shtml?tag=contentMain;contentBody

intimated that it was probably Gardner's Tongan neighbors who might be to blame. When Government officials first informed Gardner's father, they said that Deb had died but they didn't know how.

Murders are hanged in Tonga and the worst message that could come out of this was that one volunteer had murdered another and was hung for the offense. The Tongans were very upset that the Peace Corps had brought this terrible incident to their country and the news spread fast. But in America the event went unreported for 19 days.

Less than two months after the murder Priven was brought to trial in Tonga. The court room was packed with Tongans, but Mary George instructed all Peace Corps volunteers to stay away. She may have screwed up before, but she was now going to totally own the situation. She was in court every step of the way.

The prosecutor had never tired a murder case like this before and the police had bungled the investigation. They took pictures of the scene six days after the event and the place had been cleaned up. The jury was composed of seven Tongan farmers with only an elementary education. The government regulators who were to process, prosecute and evaluate the situation were basically in over their heads.

Mary George brought in a "secret weapon: Clive Edwards, the greatest criminal defense lawyer in Tonga. He was paid by the Peace Corps to defend

Priven."[2] George was going to influence the influential and do it with all the money and power she could bring to bear.

When the eye witness pointed out Priven with absolute certainty then Edwards switched to an insanity defense. The jury, who didn't speak English, had never heard of this defense before and Edwards pressed the issue by saying the Priven was "possessed by a devil." The Peace Corps was shifting the risk from personal responsibility to uncontrollable external forces.

"With the Peace Corps footing the bill, the defense even brought in Dr. Kosta Stojanovich, a psychiatrist from Hawaii with a resume a mile long. Weiss says he was the 'most educated person the Tongans have ever seen in their lives.' Stojanovich testified that Priven suffered from latent schizophrenia, with episodes triggered by stress. He said that Priven was delusional and that he thought Gardner was an evil force who had to be destroyed. But he also said that Priven had no recollection at all of having killed her."[3]

The Tongans had no money to bring in any high powered specialists. The trial lasted nine days and the verdict took just 30 minutes. Priven was declared not guilty by reason of insanity.

---

[2] http://www.cbsnews.com/stories/2005/06/15/48hours/main 702039_page4.shtml?tag=contentMain;contentBody
[3] http://www.cbsnews.com/stories/2005/06/15/48hours/main 702039_page5.shtml?tag=contentMain;contentBody

Tonga had no facilities for keeping Priven in a mental hospital and so with assurances by the United States Government that he would be held in a facility until he was no longer a threat to anyone they released him to return to Washington D.C. Back in America psychiatrists evaluated him and declared that he was not a threat and so he simply went home to Brooklyn.

The Peace Corps closed the book on the whole case and every governmental official who was involved refused to talk about it. From that point on there was simply no disclosure of any information. Priven honorably completed his service with the Peace Corps and went to work for the Government as a computer specialist. He retired in 2003 and lived an anonymous life.

CBS originally aired the story on October 23rd, 2004 and later updated it on January 24th, 2008. The program was viewed again as part of a "48 Hours" program that aired in 2011. It was titled "Lost in Paradise: Who Murdered A Beautiful Peace Corps Volunteer in Tonga?" Audiences sat transfixed as the program detailed all of the events that surrounded the case.

The original incident occurred in 1975 and the two principals involved, Deb Gardner and Dennis Priven were in their early twenties. Deb died that night while Dennis went on to live a life free from any responsibility for the terrible act.[4]

This is a stark example of how powerful systems and individuals see the world. They are very Machiavellian where the ends justify the means. Deb was sacrificed on the altar of preserving the Peace Corps, its image and its mission.

At the conclusion of the story CBS attached the following: "Today over 8,000 Peace Corps volunteers serve in 74 countries including Tonga. It's the highest number of Peace Corps volunteers in almost four decades."[5]

---

[4] http://www.cbsnews.com/stories/2005/06/15/48hours/main702039.shtml
[5] http://www.cbsnews.com/stories/2005/06/15/48hours/main 702039_page6.shtml?tag=contentMain;contentBody

Niccollo' Machiavelli

"[Niccollo'] Machiavelli was born in Florence on May 5th, 1469. In his early years he was exposed to an extremely chaotic time with popes leading armies, powerful city-states falling one after another to foreign powers, and governments changing within the space of just weeks. As a student, Machiavelli was educated by the humanist ideals of the Renaissance. Later in life Machiavelli pursued a career within the government, where he was first a clerk, then an ambassador and finally on a council responsible for diplomatic negotiations and military matters. He was placed in charge of the Florentine militia and was trusted with the protection of the city. Machiavelli did not trust mercenaries or paid armies and was much more comfortable with a citizen militia. He believed citizens would possess more loyalty and would not be motivated by money. Machiavelli was very devoted to the Florentine Republic and served it for many years."

"Originally, Machiavelli played a large role in the anti-Medici government. When they came back into power Machiavelli was arrested and charged with conspiracy. He denied having anything to do with this and was eventually released. He retired to his estate in Sant'Andrea, Percussina and began writing *The Prince* in an effort to compel the Medici government to reassess his allegiance to their political beliefs."

"Machiavelli's ideas contained in *The Prince* are relatively straight forward, as he strove to provide practical, easily understood advice to Lorenzo De'Medici, to whom the book was dedicated. He did not write *The Prince* for literary acknowledgement but alternatively wrote it to prove his proficiency on government in the western world and to offer advice on how to gain power and keep it. Machiavelli strongly believed in the requirement of a strong leader in order to maintain domination for the benefit of citizens and not for individual advancement."[6]

"The descriptions within *The Prince* have the general theme of accepting that the aims of princes, such as glory, and indeed survival, can justify the use of immoral means to achieve those ends."[7]

The following are interpretations of the most important section from "The Prince." Included are sixteen important principles for any prince to understand and utilize in maintaining power.

Selected Quotes from <u>The Prince</u>
1. Nothing is more difficult than to control change. People are by nature fickle; and it is easy to persuade them to try something new, and equally as hard to keep them from wanting to change again. Therefore, it is necessary to be prepared to

---

[6] Boyer, Josh, http://www.online-literature.com/machiavelli/prince/
[7] http://en.wikipedia.org/wiki/The_Prince

use force so they will hold to the designated course.[8]

2. A wise leader must institute compelling reasons why constituents need the status quo and the current leader in all situations and then they will be faithful always.[9]

3. It is not difficult for a prudent leader to keep the spirits of subordinates high at the beginning of a campaign and later, as long as they feel secure and provided for.[10]

4. There is nothing more unstable in human affairs than fame or power that is not supported by its own strength and resources.[11]

5. The leader must read the histories and analyze the actions of excellent executives: see how they have managed in challenging situations, examine the reasons for their successes or failures and be able to imitate the former and avoid the latter.[12]

---

[8] The Prince, Niccolo Machiavelli, Translated and edited by Angelo M. Codevilla, Yale University Press, New Haven, paperback, 1997, chapter VI, page 22
[9] ibid, chapter IX, page 39
[10] ibid, chapter X, page 41
[11] ibid, chapter XIII, page 53
[12] ibid, chapter XIV, page 55 and 56

6. A leader must be realistic and not idealistic. The former brings preservation, while the latter brings ruin. Because of this, it may require a leader to use questionable tactics when necessary.[13]

7. It is better to have the reputation as a miser which brings infamy but not hatred, than to be known as greedy which brings infamy with hatred.[14]

8. The leader must make himself feared in such a way that, if he cannot obtain love, he may at least escape hatred. To be feared and not hated can go together very well as long as he is removed from his subordinates and does not take their possessions.[15]

9. A leader needs to be as sly as a fox to recognize traps, and strong as a lion to discourage wolves. Within these constraints, a leader must maintain a reputation for good dealing, but know when to implement bad behavior when necessary.[16]

10. It brings contempt to be seen as arbitrary, lighthearted, weak, lacking courage, and indecisive: which a leader must avoid. But instead scheme to be recognized for greatness,

---

[13] ibid, chapter XV, page 57
[14] ibid, chapter XVII, page 60
[15] ibid, chapter XVII, page 62
[16] Ibid, chapter XVIII, pages 65 and 67

spiritedness, importance, strength and insisting that statements are irrevocable concerning the affairs of subordinates. Thus people will think twice either to deceive a leader or of getting around him.[17]

11. The leader, more afraid of subordinates than of competitors, must build fortresses; but the one who is more afraid of competitors than of subordinates, has no need of them.[18]

12. Nothing makes a leader so esteemed as doing great enterprises and revealing selective examples of personal success. A leader must be regarded as a lover of virtue and honor those who excel in the arts. Keep subordinates occupied with major events at convenient times of the year.[19]

13. The most important virtue is for a leader to have the wisdom to discern which ventures will come with the greatest rewards and then pursue them with courage.[20]

---

[17] Ibid, chapter XIX, page 68
[18] Ibid, chapter XX, page 80
[19] Ibid, chapter XXI, page 81 and 84
[20] Ibid, chapter XXI, page 83

14. The first impression of a leader's wisdom comes from the intellect, capability and faithfulness of key subordinates.[21]

15. Get others to understand that they do not offend by telling the truth.[22]

16. The leader who relies on fortune and luck courts failure. Success comes from diligent effort and adapting to changing times.[23]

    As one studies the principles of "The Prince" it becomes apparent that many business and political leaders have taken these concepts to heart and use them as needed. There is debate if they are ethical or even still applicable. The fact they are still actively discussed and evaluated suggests they are very much on the minds of most serious students of leadership.

    Recently, in observing leaders in action six other concepts have become visible. These don't replace Machiavelli, but in many cases compliment the ideas that he put forward. Hundreds if not thousands of examples such as that mentioned in "Tragedy in Paradise" that was offered in the first chapter of this work could be cited that demonstrate these six concepts that leaders utilize. The remainder

---

[21] ibid, chapter XXII, page 85
[22] ibid, chapter XXIII, page 87
[23] ibid, chapter XXV, page 92 and 93

of this book will focus on the six observed traits with some examples cited.

Who Are the Powerful

Who are the people that make society go and how do they operate? First we will identify who these people are, their traits and characteristics, then explore some of the techniques they employ, and finally, evaluate the ethical ramifications of those operating methods.

In his book "Designs for Fund-Raising", Harold J. Seymour identifies how people are aggregated. He says that "in any field of human activity the top 5 percent are the creative. They light the way, originate action, take the responsibility, establish the standards, create the confidence, sustain the mood, and keep things moving.

"The next 25 to 30 percent are the responsible. They are followed by the responsive that will probably respond in varying degrees if everything is right. The bottom and merging with the responsive is the inert fifth. In any campaign a third will perform as asked (the responsible ones), a third will respond under pressure and prodding, and the last third, no matter what you or anyone else does, will turn out to be mostly deadwood."[24]

This stratification of society was confirmed by Dean George Odiorn to a graduating class from the University of Utah College of Business in June of 1971. He said "There are three types of people: those

---

[24] "Designs for Fund-Raising", Harold J. Seymour, Fund-Raising Institute, Ambler, Pa, second edition, 1966, pages 4-14

that make things happen, those that know that something happened, and those that are unaware that anything happened at all."

Will and Ariel Durant state in their book, The Lessons of History, that …history has revealed that "the men who can manage men manage the men who can manage only things, and the men who can manage money manage all."[25]

Our first conclusion is that there are people who "light the way, originate action, take the responsibility, establish the standards, create the confidence, sustain the mood, and keep things moving." They make things happen and are those who don't just manage things and people, but are responsible for the allocation of resources. We identify these people as the "Movers and Shakers."

The next question is: How do these people who keep things moving function? Don Hale, a Salt Lake City businessman once said: "There [are] many rules to success but none of them work unless you do."[26] Thomas Edison supported this position by stating "Opportunity is missed by most people because it is dressed in overalls and looks like work."[27] It seems rather obvious that activity or work

---

[25] "The Lessons of History," Will and Ariel Durant, Simon and Schuster, New York, 1968, page 54
[26] "Deseret News", "Founder of Hires Big-H dies at 93," Carole Mikita, Tuesday, February 1, 2011, page B5
[27] http://thinkexist.com/quotes/thomas_alva_edison/

is fundamental, but are there certain operating practices that denote these top performers?

After observing them for many years it has become clear that not all, but many had similar characteristics they demonstrated in the performance of their duties that seemed outside the orthodoxy that is commonly taught in most business colleges. These practices are not always obvious to the casual observer and appear to be almost secret methods. We suspect they operate more by exception than by rule.

Students are taught that the world is fair, ethical, and information represents reality. This is true to a point. Women refer to the glass ceiling in a corporation they cannot penetrate to reach executive decision making status. A similar ceiling exists that separates the rank and file who are held rigidly to standards. Below this threshold employees had better conduct themselves ethically and generate information that is accurate, relevant and reliable.

Above this hierarchal ceiling is a realm in the rarified air of executive privilege. In the case of accounting information executives use special tools to "Adjust" the numbers to reflect what they want the world to see. They use the gray areas of Generally Accepted Accounting Procedures (GAAP) and other tricks that set them apart as true artists. They don't really steal from the company and stock holders, but rather manipulate the data by moving it back and forth between the income statement and balance sheet to "smooth earnings." These techniques go by a variety of names such as "Cookie Jar Accounting."

That is a term coined by Arthur Levitt, the former Chairman of the SEC in a speech that he gave in 1998.[28]

If someone uncovers this prestidigitation of data in the financial statements the defense can always be negligence, "Gee we just didn't know." It is only intentional manipulation that is fraudulent. Below this hierarchal ceiling you had better know or you will be fired, but above this point an executive is allowed to plead ignorance.

Our hypothesis is the COUSIN Theory: The masses know the rules while the creative know the exceptions. The rules are taught and reaffirmed to the rank and file, while the movers and shakers are given exemption. When someone from the "masses" breaks the rules, through intimidation, negative rewards, or punished they are brought back into compliance.

The six observable actions that separate the top tier from all the rest are explored and revealed in the following. The COUSIN is an acronym representing the first letter of each action:

C = Control the message
O = Own the Market
U = Unregulated is best
S = Shift the Risk
I = Influence the Influential
N = No Disclosure

---

[28] http://www.sec.gov/news/speech/speecharchive/1998/spch220.txt

Control the Message

Concerning the flow of information, the standard that is taught in college is the Efficient-Market Hypothesis. "The **efficient-market hypothesis (EMH)** asserts that financial markets are 'informationally efficient'".[29] There are various forms of this hypothesis, but the underlying principle is that generally it is difficult to find some arbitrage position where the price of a company is different from its intrinsic value, because of the efficiency of information.

This theory is the rule that is commonly taught and by which most assume the world functions. Movers and shakers realize that information is power and people's activations are determined by their perception of the world. Huge sums are spent on marketing and advertising to sway the public perception and it has become a very sophisticated area of study. If markets are informationally efficient then can advertising really modify people's judgments? Executives believe they can and so they attempt to control the message.

This happens in every realm, be it business, politics, and even society generally. The people who perceive themselves to be at the top will mold their communications in such a way to motivate people in the direction they want activity to follow. At the same time they will, whether through subtle or open

---

[29] http://en.wikipedia.org/wiki/Efficient-market_hypothesis

methods, marginalize or even vilify the people and message that is contrary to their position.

At the same time students are taught that information is efficient, text books do recognize the agency problem where managers do not always look out for the best interests of stockholders, but it is only briefly discusses and then dismissed. While revealing how the world really works, it so clouds the theoretical application of models that it is not factored in as a key component.

Stockholders are represented by boards of directors who are people of influence who are charged with decision making authority over management. It is often difficult for a these directors to know what is going on in a company when all the information they receive about the company comes from management. Seldom do they get independent verification that contradicts what the executive team has presented. Besides, they have to believe in the CEO they installed to run the company.

Recently, in the Financial Crisis of 2008 we saw how even the independence of financial rating agencies had been compromised and gave companies favorable ratings, even though the companies under review were embarking on very risky high leverage strategies.[30]

The first rule of every cousin executive is to control the message so that the brand and image of the company and executive team are never in

---

[30] http://www.cmht.com/news.php?NewsID=266

question. Thorstein Veblen talks about the importance of image:

Veblin's Goodwill

"Goodwill taken in its wider meaning comprises such things as established customary business relations, reputation for upright dealing, franchises and privileges, trade-marks, brands, patent rights, copyrights, exclusive use of special processes guarded by law or by secrecy, exclusive control of particular sources of materials. All these items give a differential advantage to their owners..."[31]

Maxim #1: Image and reputation of the individual and their work are the ultimate value.

One of the first rules relating to controlling the message is to have all the information available so the executive is in a position to make accurate judgements. Napoleon had a very aggressive system for collecting the information he needed to rule as effectively as he did. Will and Ariel Durant tell us:

Napoleon and Information

---

[31] "Modern Business Capital, Chapter 6 in *The Theory of Business Enterprise*" Thorstein Veblen, New York: Charles Scribner's Sons (1904): page 139.

In the 3,680 days of his imperial rule (1804-14) he was in Paris for only 955, but in these he remade France. When at home, and before 1808, he presided regularly, twice a week, over the Council of State; and then, said Las Cases (himself a member), "none of us would have been absent for the whole world. He worked hard; in his eagerness to get things done he sometimes rose at 3 A.M. to begin his working day. He expected almost as much from his administrative aides. They were always to be ready to give him precise up-to-the-hour information on any matter falling within their jurisdiction; and he judged them by the accuracy, order, readiness, and adequacy of their reports. He did not consider his day finished until he had read the memoranda and documents that almost daily came to him from the various departments of his government. He was probably the best-informed ruler in history.[32]

Maxim #2: Have all the information possible to be in a position to make accurate judgments.

Image and reputation are protected and destroyed through the messaging to, from, and about any individual and their work. Often our political leaders are masters of message manipulation. Take for example, our current president, Barak Obama

---

[32] Will and Ariel Durant, "The Age of Napoleon," MJF Books, New York, 1975, Page 250

who seldom has a town meeting or press conference that is not controlled: where the audience and participants are hand selected supporters who will be enthusiastically responsive to his message. He has learned well from all his predecessors. The following quote focuses on this controlling the message:

Presidential Message Control

It's worth pointing out that a White House's efforts to stage and control its message hasn't always proven all that shocking to the normally-jaded Beltway press. John Harris and Mark Halperin wrote a whole book partly devoted to the idea that not losing control of your message is a cardinal virtue. "[33]

Maxim #3: Never lose control of your message.

Another method of controlling the messages is to suppress any opposing views. Catherine the Great of Russia used this technique:

Catherine the Great

Disturbed by a dozen conspiracies to unseat her, and frightened by Pugachev's revolt, she was terrified by the French Revolution. She bore with it complacently when it promised to be only the overthrow of an idle

---

[33] http://www.cjr.org/feature/message_control.php

22

aristocracy and an incompetent government; but when a Paris mob forced Louis XVI and Marie Antoinette to leave Varsailles and live in the Tuileries amid an unchained populace---when the constituent Assembly declared itself supreme, and Luis consented to be merely its executive officer--- Catherine shuddered at the encouragement so given to those who sought similar actions in Russia. She allowed the clergy to forbid the publication of her once beloved Voltaire's works (1789); she herself soon proscribed all French publications; she had the busts of Voltaire removed from her chambers to a lumber room (1792). She banished the idealistic Radishchev (1700) , imprisoned the public-spirited Novikov (1792), and established an inquisitorial censorship over literature and plays. When Louis XVI and Marie Antoinette were guillotined (1793) she broke off all relations with the French government, and urged the European monarchies to form a coalition against France.[34]

Maxim #4: Suppress opposing views.

Old media outlets are rapidly changing and new methods of communication, such as the internet and cell phones are presenting new avenues for control. The following article focuses on British Petroleum and its methods:

---

[34] Will and Ariel Durant, "Rousseau and Revolution," MJF Books, New York, 1967, page 469

BP purchasing search terms

"Late last month, as the <u>controversy</u> over the <u>Gulf oil spill</u> was just heating up, BP <u>tussled</u> with the folks behind a <u>popular spoof Twitter feed</u>. Now comes word that the PR department at BP has forked over a healthy chunk of change to control the way Web users view the company. According to BP reps, the company has purchased a range of popular search terms – including "oil spill" – from Google, the most popular search engine in the US. So what does it mean to "purchase" a search term? Well, it certainly doesn't make all the negative results go away. Today, for instance, a Google search for "oil spill" returned a range of results, including a Huffington Post article and a Wikipedia entry on oil spills. But the very top result is a shaded advertisement from BP, trumpeting the company's clean-up efforts. "Learn More about How BP is Helping," the advertisement reads."[35]

Generally, the principle involves always controlling news and public relations stories. "Talking points" will be distributed to anyone who may be required to interface with any potential informational outlet. In addition to all the people within an entity, there are all the external points of interface. Traditionally, the external people hungry for news and information include: Suppliers,

---

[35] http://www.csmonitor.com/Innovation/Horizons/2010/0609/Gulf-oil-spill-To-control-message-BP-buys-search-terms-from-Google

Customers, Trade Associations, Competitors, Investors, Media Experts, Industry Analysts, Regulators, and the Academic community. New avenues of communications are always being introduced and so it is the responsibility of great leaders to stay vigilant.

Maxim#5: Stay abreast of the technologically changing ways that messages are delivered.

What do the numbers say? This is a tool that management has used very effectively through the years. If there are several division within a corporation and management has some strategic or political reason to favor one at the expense of another it is often very easy for them to allocate costs within the accounting system. This can make any division look good and another look bad.

The author had a personal experience in a major corporation that started up a new division. For several years the fledgling entity struggled to make a profit. A switch was made at the top where one VP who oversaw the expansion was replaced with another VP who had control of the accounting process. In one year-end accounting entry profits were moved from the old division to the new and it instantly became profitable. The new VP demonstrated that he was a master at management and later was promoted to be the CEO of the whole company.

In a separate corporation and with very different people it was observed how statistics could justify a position. A person was placed in charge of collecting survey information. Through a very clever crafting of the questions, respondents were lead to the correct answers. The same person who crafted the questions then tabulated and summarized the results. Conclusions were reached that justified an ideological position.

The whole process was reviewed by others who concluded that very different conclusions could be reached by wording the questions differently and consolidating the responses with a different slant.

Numerous stories such as this could be recounted from personal experience and the press. The bottom line is that if data and statistics are required to support a message, the skilled and crafty mover and shaker will find a way to justify their position.

Maxim #6: Control financial and statistical data to support the desired position.

Summary

What are the methods for controlling the message:

The techniques for controlling the message include:
Study the situation

Develop the message
Prepare talking points
Rehearse the team
Select the audience
Stage the informational event.
Control data that will justify a position

As a follow up to this, if a contrary position is presented:

Attack the message
Marginalize its importance
Coordinate collaborative opposition
Generate undermining evidence
Vilify the opponent

In summary the reality of controlling the message is to: Be prepared, coordinate the cast, stage events, while suppressing any contrary or opposing position by vilifying opponents and marginalizing their communication.

Own the Market

Students are taught that **"Competitive advantage** occurs when an organization acquires or develops an attribute or combination of attributes that allows it to outperform its competitors."[36] The emphasis is on outperforming competitors, offering a superior product or service in a fair and open marketplace. In reality many CEOs use whatever means possible to gain market advantage and domination while limiting or removing the competition.

It is critical for any company to have a franchise or proprietary position where they have some control over their market. An executive must not only develop products and services that stand out and are dominant, but they must work within the types of markets that are available to them. In his classic work "The Art of War," Sun Tzu talks about Terrain. Is it too farfetched to liken terrain to the various types of markets that a business might operate in? With a little imagination one can see the relationship. It is proposed that the first rule in owning the market is to know the characteristics of the market one is operating in:

Sun Tzu's "Art of War" modified for Business

---

[36] http://en.wikipedia.org/wiki/Competitive_advantage

1. **Accessible**: Enter before the competition with a superior brand and image, and carefully guard your relationships with suppliers. Then you will be able to compete with advantage.
2. **Entangling**: Markets which can be abandoned, but may be hard to re-enter, are called entangling. If the competition is unprepared, they may be easily displaced
3. **Temporized**: When neither competitor can gain the edge by making the first move, hold back, waiting for the competition to reveal their position to be challenged with advantage.
4. **Niche**: if first in place, then protect aggressively. If a competitor is first with a dominant market share, it may be unprofitable to enter. Only enter if the competitor is vulnerable.
5. **Exclusive**: If a priority position with a dominant brand: promote the image aggressively. If the competition has preference the only option is to entice them away from their position.
6. **Foreign**: It may be difficult to challenge a competitor that is equally resourced in an unfamiliar market. This situation must be carefully analyzed and evaluated, before any action is taken[37]

Maxim #7: Know your market.

---

[37] "The Art of War", Sun Tzu, Translated by Lionel Giles, Barnes & Noble Classics, New York, 2003, page 182-186

For the powerful, adapting to the various venues is critical. Charlemagne was a prime example of this adaptation. Extending his power by leading countless military engagements he dealt with all of his constituents as needed:

Charlemagne's Adaptation

He had now brought under his rule all the peoples between the Vistula and the Atlantic, between the Baltic and the Pyrenees, with nearly all of Italy and much of the Balkans. How could one man competently govern so vast and varied a realm? He was strong enough in body and nerves to bear a thousand responsibilities, perils, and crises, even to his sons' plotting to kill him. He had in him the blood or teachings of the wise and cautious Pepin III, and of the ruthless Charles Martel, and was something of a hammer himself. He extended their power, guarded it with firm military organization, propped it with religious sanction and ritual. He could vision large purposes, and could will the means as well as wish the ends. He could lead an army, persuade an assembly, humor the nobility, dominate the clergy, [and] rule a harem.[38]

Maxim #8: Read the markets and adapt.

---

[38] Will and Ariel Durant, "The Age of Faith," MJF Books, New York, 1950, page 462463

Once the type of market is determined, the mover and shakers will evaluate their chances for success. Napoleon suggested that once a campaign is launched it must be taken to the max.[39] And how could a discussion of market domination pass without a reference to Machiavelli.

Machiavelli's Prince

Whoever, therefore, on entering a new Princedom, judges it necessary to rid himself of enemies, to conciliate friends, to prevail by force or fraud, to make himself feared yet not hated by his subjects, respected and obeyed by his soldiers, to crush those who can or ought to injure him, to introduce change in the old order of things, to be at once severe and affable, magnanimous and liberal, to do away with a mutinous army and create a new one….can find no brighter example than in the actions of this Prince.[40]

Maxim #9: Own the market by whatever means possible.

This is not just competitive advantage, but truly methods to own the market by whatever means possible. A more recent example is the rise of

---

[39] Napoleon's Art of War, translated from the French by Lieut.-Gen. Sir G.C. D'Aguilar, C.B., Barnes & Noble Books, New York, 1995.
[40] The Prince, Niccolo Machiavelli, Barnes & Noble Books, New York, 1999, page 28

General Motors to domination in the twentieth century. One of the early obstacles was the limitation that customers found in trying to finance the purchase of one of their cars.

General Motors Acceptance Corporation (GMAC)

We got into [the financing] business…when the need for financing the distribution of automobiles first arose. Mass production brought with it the need for a broad approach to consumer financing, which the banks did not then take kindly to. They neglected---I might say they declined---to meet the need; and so some other means had to be found if the auto industry was to sell cars in large numbers.[41]

       General Motors overcame this challenge by forming their own finance company. Through this new and innovative mechanism they were able to rapidly expand their market and domination. Unfortunately, General Motors is also a classic example of a company that mismanaged its products and their markets in the late 1900s. It became old and ossified. It supposed that through controlling the message and telling people that quality was something you could advertise and that people would believe you. They never supposed they actually had to deliver. Their loss of ownership of the market is

---

[41] "My Years with General Motors," Alfred P. Sloan, Jr., Doubleday, New York, 1963, Page 302

evidence that executives didn't change with the times.

Maxim #10: Cutting edge innovation and changing with the market are critical.

It is easy to own the market if you are the only game in town and can ensure that is the case. Countries with dictatorships or even in democracies where governments regulate and restrict competition can ensure dominance. In free markets the best a company can hope for is not a monopoly, but perhaps a duopoly. The following article discusses a duopolies and their domination:

Duopolies

…there are industries with duopolies or three or four firms that have a dominant market share. Monopolies they are not, but there is plenty of room to profit when you share the whole pie with one or two other competitors. If you examine duopolistic industries today, you will also notice fantastic value creation over a period of many years. **Coca-Cola** (NYSE:KO) and **PepsiCo** (NYSE:PEP) are two great examples. Look at a chart at both companies for the past 20 years and you will see tremendous value creation not only from stock price appreciation, but from continuous dividend payments as well. When it comes to shipping packages, most choose between

---

UPS (NYSE:<u>UPS</u>) or **FedEx** (NYSE:<u>FDX</u>), another strong sign of market dominance. In the past 10 years, shares in FedEx have appreciated by over 110% - and that's not including dividend payments.[42]

Maxim #11: If you can't own the market, make sure only a few major competitors exist.

When Queen Elizabeth ascended to the thrown of England, a dominating individual of power took control of the British Empire. Will and Ariel Durant talk about her absolutism:

Queen Elizabeth I absolutism

Rarely, and reluctantly, she summoned Parliament to her financial aid, for she did not patiently bear opposition, criticism, or surveillance. She put no stock in theories of popular or parliamentary sovereignty: she believed with Homer and Shakespeare that only one head should rule---and why not hers, in which ran the blood and burned the pride of Henry VIII? She held to the divine right of kings and Queens. She imprisoned persons at her own sharp will, without trial or stated cause; and her Privy Council, acting as the Court of Star Chamber to try political offenders, suspended without appeal the rights of habeas corpus and jury trail. She punished

---

[42] http://stocks.investopedia.com/stock-analysis/2010/Stocks-That-Own-The-Market-LABS-DGX-UPS-FDX-KO-PEP0920.aspx

M.P.s who obstructed her purposes. She suggested to the local magnates who manipulated elections to Parliament that it would facilitate maters if they close candidates with no boyish notions about free speech; she wanted pounds without palaver. Her early Parliaments yielded gracefully; her middle Parliaments yielded angrily; her later Parliaments neared revolt.[43]

Maxim #12: Absolute power may be conferred by divine right.

Healthcare in the United States is a very unique case where legal regulations control the industry and access to it, but it is theoretically an open market. Every resident in the country is not covered by some form of affordable insurance and yet more is spent in the United States on healthcare than anywhere in the world. It is neither a single payer system that is in place in every other industrialized country, nor is it a market based system where prices are determined by competition.

Double digit rate increases have plagued the system for an extended period of time resulting in the consumption of nearly twenty percent of the country's gross domestic product. This is nearly double every other country with universal care. A recent article by Havighurst and Richman suggested

---

[43] Will and Ariel Durant, "The Age of Reason Begins," MJF Books, New York, 1961, page 7

that monopoly enjoyed by healthcare providers may be getting out of hand.

Healthcare and Monopoly

"...monopoly power in the hands not only of nonprofit hospitals but also of other providers or suppliers of health services or products is more, not just equally, harmful to both consumers and the general welfare than monopolies of other kinds. Therefore, we submit, mergers and consolidations and other potentially monopolistic practices of health care providers—including the very recent wave of consolidating market power around so-called accountable care organizations7—should be subject to special, not relaxed, vigilance by antitrust agencies and courts. Specifically, we observe (as, surprisingly, the antitrust agencies and economists generally have not8) that U.S.-style health insurance greatly enhances the pricing freedom of firms possessing market power in health care markets, resulting in much larger monopoly profits and much greater redistributions of wealth than would result from comparable monopoly power in markets where consumers face prices directly."[44]

---

[44]CLARK C. HAVIGHURST & BARAK D. RICHMAN, "The Provider Monopoly Problem in Health Care" 3/31/2011.
http://scholarship.law.duke.edu/cgi/viewcontent.cgi?article=2905&context=faculty_sch olarship&sei-
redir=1&referer=http%3A%2F%2Fwww.google.com%2Furl%3Fsa%3Dt%26rct%3Dj %26q%3Dhealth%2520care%2520monopoly%26source%3Dweb%26cd%3D9%26ved %3D0CGAQFjAI%26url%3Dhttp%253A%252F%252Fscholarship.law.duke.edu%25

Healthcare enjoys a unique position where regulators have been so influence through the years that markets are very controlled. Doctors have a tight grip on who can gain access to information, drugs and services. As the industrial complex gets larger even less competition is experienced and pricing is racing out of control.

Maxim 13: Influence regulators to implement restrictive controls on competition

Summary

What are the methods for owning the market?

Understand the market you operating in
Align products/services to maximize the
    market
Innovate with systems to enhance domination
Pursue with maximum effort
Influence regulators to implement restrictive
    controls on competition
Remember Machiaveli:
    rid yourself of enemies
    conciliate friends,
    prevail by force or fraud,
    make yourself feared yet not hated,

make yourself respected and obeyed by
your workforce,
crush those who could injure,
introduce change in the old order of
things,
be at once severe and affable,
magnanimous and liberal,
do away with mutinous workers and
hire new ones

In summary the reality of owning the market is to: Use whatever means possible to gain market advantage and domination while limiting or removing competition.

Unregulated is Best

Students are taught to strive for a **level playing field** [that] is a concept about fairness, not that each player has an equal chance to succeed, but that they all play by the same set of rules.[45] In most cases the role of government is to establish level playing fields through regulation. It is the belief that in "free" countries these governments represent the people: They are of the people, by the people and for the people.

Unfortunately, this is an illusion. If one were to peel back the façade, the reality is that most societies function according to egonomics where an economic condition will continue as long as the movers and shakers can profit from it.

Sports are big business in America and one would hope it is a reflection of the level playing field concept. Our suspicions that even regulators are manipulated were recently confirmed when a former NBA referee made some starting allegations.

NBA Manipulating the Referees

"According to [Tim] Donaghy, [one time NBA referee] N.B.A. executives directed referees "to manipulate games" in order to 'boost ticket sales and television ratings,' and he cited several examples.

---

[45] http://en.wikipedia.org/wiki/Level_playing_field

Although the team names were withheld, Donaghy pointed to Game 6 of the 2002 Western Conference finals as one such instance. The Los Angeles Lakers shot 40 free throws in that game — 27 in the fourth quarter — and beat Sacramento, 106-102, forcing a seventh game. The Lakers went on to win the series and beat the Nets for their third straight N.B.A. title. The Kings, their fans and many in the news media were outraged by the officiating that night. Ralph Nader, the consumer advocate, weighed in, urging Stern to conduct a review."[46]

Maxim #14: Regulators can be manipulated to profit the powerful and egocentric.

Here is a case where regulators were manipulated to benefit the movers and shakers that dominated the professional basketball market. Penetrating the veil of secrecy regarding what really goes on can be very instructive.

Companies would love to function without third party intervention or restriction that would limit or curtail carte blanche activity. In fact the ideal business is one that is totally unregulated, where executives can make decisions without someone looking over their shoulder or having to file endless reports. Most companies would rather be privately owned and avoid public reporting, but are forced to

---

[46] http://www.phillysportsforums.com/forums/showthread. php?28490-More-Donaghy-%28NBA-Ref%29-Revelations

go public because of the need for the massive amounts of investment required to grow.

Even as some companies have become huge public entities they have been able to avoid some of the regulations that others must bear. One example is the case of Fannie Mae and Freddie Mac. Although their stock is publicly traded they have received special exemption from Sarbanes-Oxley requirements and other controls. This led them into housing crisis that resulted in the problems of the economic collapse of 2008.

Regulation of Fannie Mae and Freddie Mac

"WASHINGTON — A Democratic plan to rein in the financial industry is flawed because it fails to tighten control over two large government-sponsored mortgage companies blamed for creating a demand for risky loans and inflating the housing bubble, a leading GOP senator on banking issues says. The legislation "touches nearly every corner of the economy," Alabama Sen. Richard Shelby said in the GOP weekly radio and Internet address. "But these major contributors to the crisis are left unscathed," he added, singling out Fannie Mae and Freddie Mac. 'For years, Democrats blocked meaningful reform of Fannie and Freddie, and not much has changed,' Shelby said."[47]

---

[47] http://www.huffingtonpost.com/2010/05/08/shelby-fannie-mae-freddie-mac-financial-reform_n_569113.html

Maxim #15: Aligning political goals can result in special exemption from regulation.

As part of the housing crisis of 2008 many of the regulations that were supposed to govern the market were outdated and entities were allowed to shop for the venue where regulations were most favorable. A report to congress in February of 2011 brought many of the practices to light:

Reforming America's Housing Market

An inadequate and outdated regulatory regime failed to keep the system in check: Regulatory boundaries largely unchanged from the 1930s allowed large parts of the financial system that were deeply involved in housing finance to operate with virtually no oversight. To be sure, there were some problems that arose from violations of the law. In many cases, however, weak and fragmented regulation and enforcement also allowed lenders to "shop" for weaker oversight and drove deteriorating standards in lending practices. Securitizers and investors could essentially opt-out of the parts of the system with heavier regulation and use whatever underwriting practices they saw fit. Other actors in the system

---

were allowed to avoid consistent regulation and choose favorable jurisdictions.[48]

Maxim #16: *A complex and outdated regulatory environment allows for manipulation.*

A personal example from the author highlights another problem with regulation. I was acting as a consultant for a government agency charged with oversight of a particular industry. After several years dealing with rate cases and reviews it became apparent the agency wanted a good working relationship with those they were regulating.

On one occasion I was asked to evaluate the viability of an entity and reported back that it was in violation and did not meet the threshold of performance that was required. The agency wanted me to submit a report recommending the entity be shut down and loose its license. I responded that I could only report on what I found and the agency was responsible for taking the necessary action of closing the entity.

My contact at the agency said that if they were to initiate such an action they could be sued and their legal counsel advised them not to take that action. They wanted to shift the burden of potential legal action to me as the consultant. It became apparent

---

[48] Reforming America's Housing Finance Market, A Report to Congress, February 2011, http://portal.hud.gov/hudportal/documents/huddoc?id=housingfinmarketreform.pdf

that agencies have a very difficult time being heavy handed for any number of constraints.

The press continues to expose all levels of government and institutional regulators who are too close to those they regulate.

Maxim #17: Regulators are reluctant to be the bad guy and are too close to those they regulate.

Another example of companies fighting for an unregulated position is the recent passage of Healthcare reform. As of Oct 2010 there had been numerous major corporations that had received waivers from compliance to the new law. When they threatened to drop coverage for their employees the government backed off and allowed them to continue unregulated.

Waivers Aim at Talk of Dropping Health Coverage

As Obama administration officials put into place the first major wave of changes under the health care legislation, they have tried to defuse stiffening resistance — from companies like <u>McDonald's</u> and some insurers — by granting dozens of waivers to maintain even minimal coverage far below the new law's standards. The waivers have been issued in the last several weeks as part of a broader strategic effort to stave off threats by some health insurers to

---

abandon markets, drop out of the business altogether or refuse to sell certain policies.[49]

Maxim #18: Size of operations and threats of non-support can compromise regulators.

But if a company is regulated, what can it do beyond threatening the government. Barry Minkow went to prison for manipulating the finances of ZZZZ Best corporation.

Barry Minkow grew up in the San Fernando Valley of California. At the age of nine his mother got him a job in the carpet-cleaning business she worked in. When he was fifteen he started his own carpet cleaning business in his parent's garage. At first, meeting basic expenses was a struggle so he turned to creative financial maneuvers to keep things going such as check kiting and fraudulent credit card charges.

Moving money between banks required that he grow much larger very fast, but he was limited by the basic business of carpet-cleaning. With the help of an insurance claims adjuster he fabricated an ancillary business of building restorations. Fake documents were crafted to justify a huge revenue stream from this bogus business.

As Minkow moved money around from bank to bank the whole enterprise became a massive Ponzi

---

[49] http://www.nytimes.com/2010/10/07/business/07insure.html

scheme where he was continually "Robbing Peter to Pay Paul." Finally, to get the money he needed to pay old claims he took the business public in 1986.

The auditors failed to visit any of his restoration sites that were the main source of his income and growth. He manipulated the auditors by having them and their wives over for dinner at his mansion. He would use this personal connection with their families to his benefit. He also told the auditors that if they went to the sites they could potentially threaten his business with the loss of clients.

Another ploy he used was to challenge the auditors by saying that another audit firm would love to have this account and how could they doubt a company that had some of the biggest names in the legal field as their attorneys. Another tactic he used was to divert their attention by asking for their advice on critical business decision.

Consequently, the auditors were compromised and did not perform all the required audit steps necessary. They relied on single sheets of paper that represented some of the largest restoration jobs in history. Minkow had learned the rules of the game to escape regulatory oversight. When the fraud was finally discovered hundreds of millions were lost by investors that had relied on compromised data.[50]

---

[50] http://books.google.com/books?id=VLxvUV8xFsgC&pg=PA84&lpg=PA84&dq=ZZZZ+best+manipulated+auditors&source=bl&ots=ZIIps-B0zC&sig=2MrfAKQfUfMO-QwkREELxuy-tFA&hl=en&ei=_l9ITZjsKYWasAOb6ezEAg&sa=X&oi=book_resul

Maxim #19: Multiple techniques can be used to intimidate and compromise regulators.

Summary

What are the methods for unregulated is best:

Opt to be a private entity instead of public
Seek favored status to fulfill bigger mission
Go over regulators heads for preferential treatment
If large, threaten regulators to ease restrictions

In summary the reality of unregulated is best is: Find ways to function without third party intervention or restriction that would limit or curtail carte blanche activity.

_____

t&ct=result&resnum=3&ved=0CCMQ6AEwAg#v=onepage&q=ZZZ
Z%20best%20manipulated%20auditors&f=false

47

Shift the Risk

Students are instructed that in its purest sense there is a **Risk-Return Trade-off**: The basic concept that higher expected returns accompany greater risk, and vice versa.[51] The orthodoxy states that risk can be measured and the expected return can be adjusted to compensate for the increased possibility of default. So shifting the risk is theoretically dealt with by demanding higher returns. But there are additional techniques that movers and shakers know.

They know to avoid excessive risk, but when damages result, use techniques to insure others will bear the burden and pay the penalty. This may sound a lot like the old trick of "passing the buck" and it well may be. This technique was probably learned when children would always point to someone else and say "I didn't do it." In business the rule is never take the blame for anything and always take the credit.

One of the greatest movers and shakers in history was Thales of Miletus. Aristotle was so captivated by the story of how Thales acquired great wealth that he referred to the incident over two hundred years later.

Thales and The Olive Presses

---

[51] http://financial-dictionary.thefreedictionary.com/Risk-Return+Tradeoff

"There is the anecdote of Thales the Milesian and his financial device, which involves a principle of universal application, but is attributed to him on account of his reputation for wisdom. He was reproached for his poverty, which was supposed to show that philosophy was of no use. According to the story, he knew by his skill in the stars while it was yet winter that there would be a great harvest of olives in the coming year; so, having a little money, he gave deposits for the use of all the olive-presses in Chios and Miletus, which he hired at a low price because no one bid against him. When the harvest-time came, and many were wanted all at once and all of a sudden, he let them out at any rate which he pleased, and made a quantity of money. Thus he showed the world that philosophers can easily be rich if they like, but that ambition is of another sort. He is supposed to have given a striking proof of his wisdom, but, as I was saying, his device for getting wealth is of universal application, and is nothing but the creation of a monopoly."[52]

Maxim #20: Reduce risk by using personal or inside information.

Almost every principle of the COUSIN theory is demonstrated here, but in particular the avoidance of risk is pronounced. In the first place Thales

---

[52] Introduction to Aristotle, Edited by Richard McKeon, Random House, The Modern Library, New York, 1947, Page 573-574

avoided risk by having advanced information about the coming season. Then to minimize risk he purchased options for not much money so that he could either walk away or exercise his contract and use the olive presses. To additionally minimize risk he secured all of the presses in town, thus creating a monopoly and ensuring the freedom to price and not be constrained by competition. Using advanced information and the creation of a monopoly minimized risk while the use of options shifted the risk to others.

Advanced information is so critical that the classic story of Nathan Rothschild is a pointed example:

The Rothschild Information system

"Nathan had promised prizes for the most speedy supply of news to boats sailing between England and the Continent. He also instructed his agents throughout the world to give him the earliest possible report regarding the outcome of the expected conflict. Nathan's arrangements worked perfectly for the battle of Waterloo. [His agent] entered the British capital very early in the morning of June 20, and immediately reported to Nathan, who conveyed the news of victory to…the British government. The government was at first skeptical. Nathan was alleged to have exploited the news on the stock exchange,

---

> thus at one stroke creating the enormous fortunes of the Rothschild's."[53]

Jacob Fugger, the great European capitalist of the fifteenth century was a master at reducing risk. His technique was to acquire advanced information. He worked closely with the royal courts of Europe, lending them money and placing runners at key strategic places. When kings would make any major financial decisions, Fugger's runners would immediately head to Augsburg, Germany and the Fugger bank to relate the news. With this advanced information Jacob was able to reduce his losses and risk.[54]

Maxim #21: Putting systems in place to gain advanced information reduces risk.

But we are talking about shifting the risk. A lot of companies try to shift the risk by purchasing insurance, options, or futures. These contracts can often remove risk and make aggressive investment decisions less likely to default. The trouble comes when not everything acts like it should.

---

[53] "The Rise of the House of Rothschild," Count Egon Caesar Corti, Western Islands, Boston, 1928, page 156-157
[54] "Jacob Fugger The Rich," Jacob Strieder, Translated by Mildred L. Hartsough, Edited by N.S.B. Gras, Archon Books, New York, 1966

Recently, we have had two great examples of shifting risk. One is the case of Long Term Capital Management the Hedge Fund that attempted to raise billions of dollars of investments to explore the use of the Black-Sholes model. They would invest over three billion dollars in the late 1990s all around the world. The directors of the scheme were some of the brightest minds in finance and for several years the returns were in the 40% per year range.

Long-Term Capital Management

THE financial crisis is a result of many bad decisions, but one of them hasn't received enough attention: the 1998 bailout of the Long-Term Capital Management hedge fund. If regulators had been less concerned with protecting the fund's creditors, our current problems might not be quite so bad. Long-Term Capital was advised by finance quants, or quantitative analysts, who made a number of unsound, esoteric bets, including investments in interest rate derivatives.

When Russia's inability to pay its debts roiled global markets, the fund, saddled with high-leverage and off-balance-sheet obligations, was near collapse. Because Long-Term Capital owed large sums to banks and other financial institutions, the Federal Reserve Bank of New York organized a consortium of companies to buy it out and cover the debts. Alan Greenspan, then the Fed chairman, eased monetary policy to restart capital markets, which were starting to freeze up. Long-Term Capital's shareholders were wiped out, but none of the creditors took losses.[55]

Things were wonderful for LTCM until the Thai real estate market collapsed and then the Russians defaulted on some of their obligations. With thirty times leverage LTCM was suddenly way over extended and no amount of financial modeling could save them. The US government had to facilitate a bail out of the company. The executives were successful in the ultimate shifting of risk, to the payer of last resort.

How like the LTCM crisis of the 1990s was the AIG and Credit Default Swaps fiasco of the 2000s. The swaps were supposed to cover any risk, but when unforeseen real estate losses and excessive leverage at major banks created another potential collapse in the financial markets, the US government entered once again to bail out the principles. Every good executive will find a way to shift the risk to someone else.

Government Bailouts

(CBS/ AP) "Democrats and Republicans alike pummeled Treasury Secretary Timothy Geithner on Wednesday over his role in the $180 billion bailout

---

[55] http://www.nytimes.com/2008/12/28/business/economy/28 view.html

of insurance giant AIG Inc., venting public anger over Wall Street's return to prosperity while 10 percent of Americans are still jobless. Geithner, one of the original architects of the government's 2008 response to the financial crisis as president of the Federal Reserve Bank of New York, defended the use of taxpayer money as necessary to head off "potentially catastrophic damage to the economy. In effect, the taxpayers were propping up the hollow shells of AIG by stuffing it with money. And the rest of Wall Street came by and looted the corpse," committee chairman Edolphus Towns, D-N.Y., told Geithner."[56]

Maxim #22: If an entities failure will impact the stability of the whole, outside funds will be marshaled to rescue and save the struggling party.

Perhaps the master of shifting the risk or blame is Barak Obama. "President Obama has passed the buck to others – mainly George W. Bush – for problems that characterize his presidency, suggesting time and again that his own policies are not to blame for his difficulties and he is simply doing the best that can be done with the cards he was dealt.[57]"

---

[56] http://www.cbsnews.com/stories/2010/01/27/business/main6146528.shtml
[57] http://www.whitehousedossier.com/2012/03/23/president-obamas-hall-blame/

Oil Prices (Mar 2012): "The key thing that is driving higher gas prices is actually the world's oil markets and uncertainty about what's going on in Iran and the Middle East, and that's adding a $20 or $30 premium to oil prices."

Solyndra (Mar 2012): "Obviously, we wish Solyndra hadn't gone bankrupt. Part of the reason they did was because the Chinese were subsidizing their solar industry and flooding the market in ways that Solyndra couldn't compete. But understand, this was not our program per se. Congress–Democrats and Republicans–put together a loan guarantee program."

Afghanistan (Mar 2012): "When I came into office there has been drift in the Afghanistan strategy, in part because we had spent a lot of time focusing on Iraq instead. Over the last three years we have refocused attention on getting Afghanistan right. Would my preference had been that we started some of that earlier? Absolutely. But that's not the cards that were dealt. We're now in a position where, given our starting point, we're making progress."

Iran (Mar 2012): "When I took office, the efforts to apply pressure on Iran were in tatters. Iran had gone from zero centrifuges spinning to thousands, without facing broad pushback from the world. In the region, Iran was ascendant."

The Economy (Feb 2012): "We've made sure to do everything we can to dig ourselves out of this incredible hole that I inherited."

The Deficit (Nov 2011): "We thought that it was entirely appropriate for our governments and our agencies to try to root out waste, large and small, in a systematic way. Obviously, this is even more important given the deficits that we've inherited and that have grown as a consequence of this recession."

The Debt (Aug 2011): "Look, we do have a serious problem in terms of debt and deficit, and much of it I inherited when I showed up."

Unemployment (May 2011): "We inherited the worst recession since the Great Depression, a banking system on the verge of meltdown. We had lost 4 million jobs by the time I was sworn in and would then lose another 4 million in the few months right after I was sworn in before our economic policies had a chance to take root."

The BP Gulf Oil Spill (Mar 2010): "In this instance, the oil industry's cozy and sometimes corrupt relationship with government regulators meant little or no regulation at all. When Secretary Salazar took office, he found a Minerals and Management Service that had been plagued by corruption for years — this was the agency charged with not only providing permits, but also enforcing laws governing oil drilling."

The Election of Sen. Scott Brown (R-Mass.) (Jan 2010): "The same thing that swept Scott Brown into office swept me into office. People are angry, and they're frustrated. Not just because of what's happened in the last year or two years, but what's happened over the last eight years."

Anti-Americanism (Sep 2009): "I took office at a time when many around the world had come to view America with skepticism and distrust. Part of this was due to misperceptions and misinformation about my country. Part of this was due to opposition to specific policies, and a belief that on certain critical issues, America has acted unilaterally, without regard for the interests of others. And this has fed an almost reflexive anti-Americanism, which too often has served as an excuse for collective inaction."

The Financial Crisis (Jun 2009): "We inherited a financial crisis unlike any that we've seen in our time. This crisis crippled private capital markets and forced us to take steps in our financial system — and with our auto companies — that we would not have otherwise even considered."

It is easy to pick on Barak Obama because he is the man of the hour. He is simply a very graphic example of what every power player knows: you never accept blame for anything that is going on around you. You always shift the blame and the risk.

Maxim #23: Shift the blame whenever possible.

Summary

What are the methods for shifting the risk:

Phase	Technique
Avoidance	Advanced Information Intimidation Insider; Spy Network; and Cross Checking
Responsibility	Appearance of Innocence Find Scapegoats (shift the blame) Shell Games (hide the blame) Claim Negligence (not Intentional)
Recovery	Insurance and options Show Importance to the System for bailouts

In summary the reality of shifting the risk is: Avoid excessive risk, but when damages result, use techniques to insure others will bear the burden and pay the penalty.

Influence the Influential

Leadership: the process of social influence in which one person can enlist the support of others to accomplish tasks.[58] This is the standard business school way of dealing with training the rank and file. It used to be training in management that has now been rebadged to focus on leadership. Somehow we have moved from command and control to persuasion. The reality of functioning in the mover and shaker world is that other people of influence must find advantage in support and danger in opposition. They strive to understand what motivates other people of power and subtly communicate and reinforce rewards and punishments.

The rule here is to cultivate influence and then know how to use it. Influence comes in a variety of ways. Family alliances and strategic marriages are some of the most obvious that have been practiced throughout history. Another way is through some form of control. A few ways to control others is through (1) Superstition and or religious right; (2) Wealth and Physical power; (3) Withholding information; (4) Confusion and complication; and (5) Regulation, laws, and rules.

Every great executive builds influence and then subtly wields it to promote corporate enterprise and personal power. Industry associations, vendors, and customers can be influenced through special

---

[58] http://en.wikipedia.org/wiki/Leadership

agreements, premiums, and access. Influence extends to controlling the media and the kinds of news that is distributed about a company. It is found as the company uses political contributions to control how politicians make laws that may affect their industry and even the company itself. Banking and the access to capital is another target of influence.

One of the greatest examples of influence was the banker J. P. Morgan. Long before there was a federal reserve bank he was the most powerful financier in America. Some say he rescued the American financial system in the great Panic of 1907. As a reward for his efforts he demanded and received privilege from President Theodore Roosevelt.

J. P. Morgan and the Panic of 1907

The Panic of 1907, also known as the 1907 Bankers' Panic, was a financial crisis that occurred in the United States when the New York Stock Exchange fell close to 50% from its peak the previous year. Panic occurred, as this was during a time of economic recession, and there were numerous runs on banks and trust companies. The 1907 panic eventually spread throughout the nation when many state and local banks and businesses entered into bankruptcy. The crisis was triggered by the failed attempt in October 1907 to corner the market on stock of the United Copper Company. The panic may have deepened if not for the intervention of financier

J. P. Morgan, who pledged large sums of his own money, and convinced other New York bankers to do the same, to shore up the banking system. At the time, the United States did not have a central bank to inject liquidity back into the market."[59]

Maxim #24: Share the resources you possess to gain favor with influential people.

Influence is not only among business executives, but the American government has used this tool with dictators across the world to work in their behalf.

New York Times: Dancing With Dictators, Published: September 01, 2002

For a nation that honors democracy and freedom, the United States has a nasty habit of embracing foreign dictators when they seem to serve American interests. It is one of the least appealing traits of American foreign policy. Like his predecessors, President Bush is falling for the illusion that tyrants make great allies. If Mr. Bush is not careful, Washington will be mopping up for years from the inevitable foreign policy disasters that come of befriending autocrats who maintain a stranglehold on their own people. When unsavory governments control strategic

---

[59] http://en.wikipedia.org/wiki/Panic_of_1907

locations or resources, the impulse to join hands with them can be irresistible. In some cases, there may appear to be no practical alternative. It would have been much more difficult to dislodge the Taliban and Al Qaeda from Afghanistan without the cooperation of Pakistan's military ruler, Gen. Pervez Musharraf. Washington's longstanding ties to the Saudi royal family have ensured a steady flow of oil to the West for most of the last 60 years.[60]

Maxim #25: Don't make judgments about influential people, but use the benefit they provide.

How many times have we seen dictators in repressive regimes supported by the United States with billions in aid simply because they are friendly? What does friendly mean? Usually, it means that American corporations receive some economic benefit from the relationship.

Gratuities, kickbacks, enticements, and perks have all been used to ingratiate powerful and influential individuals for favors throughout history. Occasionally, someone will get caught and is not able to be protected from public embarrassment and scrutiny. One was Steven Rattner:

Steven Rattner and Influence Peddling

---

[60] http://www.nytimes.com/2002/09/01/opinion/dancing-with-dictators.html

A prominent Wall Street financier has agreed to pay $10 million to settle influence-peddling allegations with the U.S. state of New York. Investment banker Steven Rattner agreed to pay the money and refrain for five years from doing business with managers of the fund that provides assistance to retired state government workers. Rattner is best known as the official in the administration of U.S. President Barack Obama who helped oversee the reorganization of the country's auto industry during the height of the world economic recession. In the New York case, Cuomo alleged that Rattner traded favors with officials so that he could arrange investments connected to the state's $125 billion pension fund.[61]

Maxim #26: Trading favors is a delicate process that may be highly risky.

Professor Thomas D. Dee II, professor of organizational behavior at Stanford University's Graduate School of Business authored a book titled "Power: Why Some People Have It---and Others Don't." His concepts were summarized in a Wall Street Journal article by Jeffrey Pfeffer:

Power: Why Some People Have It---and Others Don't by Thomas D. Dee II

[61] http://blogs.voanews.com/breaking-news/2010/12/30/wall-street-financier-settles-influence-peddling-case-for-10-million/

Many promising executives derail sometime during their careers, often because they weren't very good at office politics.

Not playing the political game is often seen as a good thing, even a badge of honor. Some managers see it as proof of their integrity. They are going to succeed because of job performance alone.

They couldn't be more wrong. Research finds that a person's political skills are key to building a successful career---for the good of both themselves and their company. When talented executives combine a knowledge of what their company needs with an ability to get things done, everyone benefits. Conversely, when a promising career falters because of poor political skills, companies have to spend time and money finding a replacement, and performance suffers in the meantime.

Being politically savvy is not about pushing others down or being untruthful to advance your own cause. Instead, it means building networks---relationships---with people inside and outside your company who can provide useful information and assistance. It means not picking fights over issues that aren't critical. It means informing others in the company about your contributions and accomplishments, and asking for advice and help, particularly from those senior to you. Self-serving? Sure. But there's nothing wrong with that. If you are going to make a difference, you need to have power.[62]

Maxim #27: A person's political skills are key to building a successful career.

A wise person once said that to deal with people and perhaps to influence them you need to understand what motivates them. There have been a lot of management gurus who have addressed this subject including Abraham Maslow:

Maslow's Hierarchy of Needs

Maslow's hierarchy of needs is often portrayed in the shape of a pyramid, with the largest and most fundamental levels of needs at the bottom, and the need for self-actualization at the top.[1][6]

The most fundamental and basic four layers of the pyramid contain what Maslow called "deficiency needs" or "d-needs": esteem, friendship and love, security, and physical needs. With the exception of the most fundamental (physiological) needs, if these "deficiency needs" are not met, the body gives no physical indication but the individual feels anxious and tense. Maslow's theory suggests that the most basic level of needs must be met before the individual will strongly desire (or focus motivation upon) the

---

[62] Jeffrey Pfeffer, "Don't Dismiss Office Politics---Teach It," Wall Street Journal, Monday, October 24, 2011, page R6

secondary or higher level needs. Maslow also coined the term Metamotivation to describe the motivation of people who go beyond the scope of the basic needs and strive for constant betterment.[7] Metamotivated people are driven by B-needs (Being Needs), instead of deficiency needs (D-Needs).

The human mind and brain are complex and have parallel processes running at the same time, so many different motivations from different levels of Maslow's pyramid usually occur at the same time. Maslow was clear about speaking of these levels and their satisfaction in terms such as "relative" and "general" and "primarily", and says that the human organism is "dominated" by a certain need[8], rather than saying that the individual is "only" focused on a certain need at any given time. So Maslow acknowledges that many different levels of motivation are likely to be going on in a human all at once. His focus in discussing the hierarchy was to identify the basic types of motivations, and the order that they generally progress as lower needs are reasonably well met.[63]

Later, others weighed in on the subject of motivation, such as Frederick Herzberg. He had a motivation-hygiene theory:

Frederick Herzberg's Motivation-Hygiene Theory

[63] http://en.wikipedia.org/wiki/Maslow's_hierarchy_of_needs

The Two-factor theory (also known as **Herzberg's motivation-hygiene theory** and **Dual-Factor Theory**) states that there are certain factors in the workplace that cause job satisfaction, while a separate set of factors cause dissatisfaction. It was developed by Frederick Herzberg, a psychologist, who theorized that job satisfaction and job dissatisfaction act independently of each other. The following table presents the top seven factors causing dissatisfaction and the top six factors causing satisfaction, listed in the order of higher to lower importance.

The factors leading to Satisfaction are: (1) Achievement; (2) Recognition; (3) Work itself; (4) Responsibility; (5) Advancement; and (6) Growth.

The factors leading to dissatisfaction are: (1) Company policy; (2) Supervision; (3) Relationship with boss; (4) Work conditions; (5) Salary; (6) Relationship with peers; and (7) Security.[64]

Whatever the basic principles of motivation are, the power person will understand what drives a person and work to that end. It may not always be money and power, but might be recognition, religion, or esteem. It might even be a passion for a sporting team or franchise.

Maxim #28: Know what motivates others.

---

[64] http://en.wikipedia.org/wiki/Two-factor_theory

Summary

The reality of functioning in the mover and shaker world is that other people of influence must find advantage in support and danger in opposition.

No Disclosure

Every good accounting student knows that **Adequate Disclosure** is a basic tenant of accounting where: Financial Statements and their accompanying notes should cover all pertinent data believed essential to the reader's understanding of the firm's financial position.[65]

To every business student who takes an accounting class the world of reporting is very systematic and precise. It usually comes as a shock when they learn later that there is a lot of room for estimation and the selection of various alternative forms of accounting for various transactions.

All major publicly traded corporations must file extensive financial reports to the Securities and Exchange Commission disclosing the most intimate of details. Even in light of this movers and shakers at the top find ways to refrain from disclosing any critical information, but if required then make it sufficiently confusing to mask the real meaning.

Consider the case of Enron:

Enron's Disclosures

Overall, Enron failed to disclose facts that were important for an understanding of the substance of

---

[65] http://www.businessdictionary.com/definition/adequate-disclosure.html

the transactions. The Company did disclose that there were large transactions with entities in which the CFO had an interest. Enron did not, however, set forth the CFO's actual or likely economic benefits from these transactions and, most importantly, never clearly disclosed the purposes behind these transactions or the complete financial statement effects of these complex arrangements. The disclosures also asserted without adequate foundation, in effect, that the arrangements were comparable to arm's-length transactions.[66]

Maxim #29: Disclosing part of the story may be as good as no disclosure at all.

Public officials are not immune from being less than transparent. The recent Health Care legislation is a prime example of smoke and mirrors that resulted in a final product.

President Obama and Transparency

(CBS) President Obama wants the final negotiations on health care reform - a reconciliation of the House and Senate versions of the bill - put on a fast track, even if that means breaking an explicit campaign promise. "The House and Senate plan to put together the final health care reform bill behind closed doors according to an agreement by top Democrats," House

---

[66] http://www.famurrell.com/Enron-Disclosure%20Issues.htm

Speaker Nanci Pelosi said today at the White House. The White House is on board with that, too, reports CBS News political correspondent Chip Reid. Press Secretary Robert Gibbs stressed today that "the president wants to get a bill to his desk as quickly as possible."

Back when Republicans controlled Congress and George W. Bush was in the White House, it was Democrats who angrily complained about secret backroom deals. Now the roles are reversed. "The negotiations are obviously being done in secret and the American people really just want to know what they are trying to hide," said Rep. Tom Price, R-Ga.[67]

Maxim #30: Backroom deals should never be transparent.

One of the largest power groups in the world are banks that control vast sums of money. In the late 1990s restrictions were removed from banks to open up more competition. Commercial banks and investment banks were allowed to merge their activities. At the same time banks began aggressively trading in derivatives like options, swaps, and futures.

---

[67] http://www.cbsnews.com/stories/2010/01/06/eveningnews/main6064298.shtml

71

Along the way to the economic meltdown of 2008 restrictions were removed from the largest banks in America so they could extend their leverage or debt to 40 to 1 from the customary 12 to 1. When the economy turned down the banks were all in danger of failing.

Many have been critical of the banks and their failure to disclose the aggressive activity they have been pursuing in the derivative area. A recent article discussed some of the issues:

Bank's Derivative Risk Disclosure

Some on Wall Street call it a "sensible" approach. "The more you disclose, the more you get Washington's lawmakers excited, and there is more talk of regulation," a Geneva-based hedge fund manager told his partners at a conference last week. "Without trades in over-the-counter currency forwards, interest rate swaps, commodity swaps, structured products and equity puts, the share-price outlook for all major banks will remain subdued, recovery regardless." Senior risk managers from Credit Suisse (CS) and Union Bank of Switzerland (UBS) who were attending the conference were in complete agreement.

According to Bloomberg (October 16, 2009), "the top five U.S. commercial banks, including JP Morgan (JPM), Goldman Sachs (GS) and Bank of America (BAC), were on track through the second

---

quarter to earn more than $35 billion this year trading unregulated derivative contracts, according to a review of company filings with the Federal Reserve and people familiar with the banks' income sources." In other words, income from OTC derivatives is an integral and influential component of bank performance, particularly in an environment where the adequacy of loan delinquency provisions is still being debated.

But if Rep. Barney Frank has his way, a significant portion of that derivatives income will be eliminated by mid-2010. The Chairman of the House Financial Services Committee has been blaming OTC derivatives, including credit default swaps and collateralized debt obligations, for last year's financial meltdown. Rep. Frank's initiatives may force a move of much of the $600 trillion OTC market to exchanges or similar regulated systems. "Transparency is the key word," a former SEC director declared on CNBC yesterday. "Let those who are buying these derivatives (i.e. corporations) know the real value of these deals." But why can't transparency be achieved now, today, by expanding disclosure on bank financial statements?

Quite clearly, the fair value measurement standards (per SFAS 157) adopted by banks provide a "framework" for making qualitative distinctions between various derivative contracts; however, the FSAS 157-related disclosure is not a substitute for a comprehensive risk analysis. For example, in theoretical terms, the most profitable OTC contracts for banks are those which reference emerging market assets (currencies, interest rates and commodities) and those which are long-dated (maturity). What is the total face value of such "exotic" contracts on the books of Citigroup (C), Goldman Sachs (GS) or Morgan Stanley (MS)? As another example, the fastest-growing business in the derivatives complex is equity-index insurance. How many long-dated index puts have been sold by Wall Street's majors?

Regardless of the sophistication achieved in hedge techniques, the measurement of risk at liquidation on exotics is a highly subjective exercise. "It does not matter if you move these exotics to a regulated exchange, the systemic risk component will stay intact," a Citibank treasury official explained. "Besides, a fair amount of the OTC deals are done through foreign branches or offshore entities, so Barney Frank's efforts to engineer more regulation are counter-productive."[68]

Many attempts have been made to force banks to disclose, but they have so much money and power, can employ the best lobbyist of congress, and can pretty well dictate what rules are passed for disclosure. The old adage "He who has the gold makes the rules" still prevails.

---

[68] http://seekingalpha.com/article/167063-banks-failing-to-disclose-derivatives-risk

Maxim #31: Powerful money interests can influence congress to prevent disclosure.

Summary

The techniques for non-disclosure are to:

Withhold information
Speak in Generalities
Shift the focus
Cloud the situation
Complicate the data

In summary, no disclosure or transparency means to: Find ways to refrain from disclosing any critical information, but if required then make it sufficiently confusing to mask the real meaning.

A Case Study

These six principles can be demonstrated over and over again:

Control the message
Own the market
Unregulated
Shift the risk
Influence the influential
No disclosure

One interesting case is college football, one of the biggest businesses in the United States.

NEW YORK (CNNMoney.com)

The richest college football programs got richer in 2010, pocketing more than $1 billion in profits for the first time.

The profit for the 68 teams that play in the six major conferences was up 11% from the prior school year, according to a CNNMoney analysis of figures filed by each school with the Department of Education.

In the school year that ended in 2010, the vast majority of the schools in one of these deep-pocketed conferences posted a profit. Four of them broke even and only one -- Wake Forest -- reported a loss.

On average, each team earned $15.8 million last year, or well over $1 million per game.

They posted that jump in combined profit even though revenue rose by only 6% to $2.2 billion. That means the schools had a combined profit margin of 49%, enough to make any pro team owner green with envy.[69]

One of the most dominating conferences in college football is the Big Ten. In a Forbes article published in January of 2011 a quick look at the football related numbers reveals:

"Here's a quick breakdown of the **averages** [2009-2010] for each category (the totals would be misleading because the SEC has twelve teams and the Big Ten only eleven)[70]:"

	Football Revenue	Football Expenses	Football Profit
SEC	$49,900,780	$19,954,052	$29,946,728
Big Ten	$40,578,173	$17,886,754	$22,691,418

Protecting the Big Ten football franchise is critical and the movers and shakers know it. They simply do not want the masses to know what is really going on. They have secret deals and excessive

---

[69] http://money.cnn.com/2010/12/29/news/companies/college_football_dollars/index.htm
[70] http://www.forbes.com/sites/sportsmoney/2011/01/30/how-the-big-ten-stacks-up-against-the-sec-in-sports-revenues/

compensation packages that would cause considerable backlash. One of our favorite cases of lack of transparency is college football's Bowl Championship Series. This is a pact by the most powerful movers and shakers of college football to keep the dollars to themselves. If one were to examine the Big Ten conference in the 2010 year it becomes quite interesting.

If overall records are the only thing that mattered then all but three of the eleven teams in the Big Ten would have more than six wins for the season and qualify for a post season bowl game. This is what everyone focused on and although the reality was available, it was somehow masked by the controlling forces of the media and the NCAA.

On the surface it looks like the big-10 was a dominant football conference, but after some digging: If games against non-BCS teams were not counted then only three of the big-10 teams would have 6 or more wins and qualified for bowls.

TEAM (School)	CONF	OVER-ALL	BCS games
Ohio State	7-1	11-1	8-1
Michigan State	7-1	11-1	8-1
Wisconsin	7-1	11-1	8-1
Iowa	4-4	7-5	5-5
Illinois	4-4	7-5	5-4
Penn State	4-4	7-5	4-5
Michigan	3-5	7-5	5-5

Northwestern	3-5	7-5	5-5
Purdue	2-6	4-8	2-7
Minnesota	2-6	3-9	2-7
Indiana	1-7	5-7	1-7

If games against non-BCS school were eliminated from consideration then only three of the teams had more than six victories and winning records. Without considering fundamental shortcoming and counting all games then eight teams went on to bowl games and received substantial paydays.

Summary

The following chart may help to summarize the various points just discussed:

	Ideal	Reality
Control the Message	The **efficient-market hypothesis** (**EMH**) asserts that <u>financial markets</u> are "informationally efficient".	Support and sustain a primary point of view while suppressing any contrary or opposing position. Vilify and marginalize opponents.
Own the Market	**Competitive advantage** occurs when an organization acquires or develops an attribute or combination of attributes that allows it to outperform its competitors.	Use whatever means possible to gain market advantage and domination while limiting or removing competition.

Unregulated Is best	A **level playing field** is a <u>concept</u> about <u>fairness</u>, not that each player has an equal chance to succeed, but that they all play by the same set of rules.	Function without third party intervention or restriction that would limit or curtail carte blanche activity.
Shift the risk	**Risk-Return Trade-off**: The basic concept that higher expected <u>returns</u> accompany greater <u>risk</u>, and vice versa.	Avoid excessive risk, but when damages result, use techniques to insure others will bear the burden and pay the penalty.
Influence the influential	**Leadership:** the process of social influence in which one person can enlist the support of others to accomplish tasks.	Other people of influence must find advantage in support and danger in opposition.

No Disclosure	**Adequate Disclosure**: Financial Statements and their accompanying notes should cover all pertinent data believed essential to the reader's understanding of the firm's financial position.	Refrain from disclosing any critical information, but if required then make it sufficiently confusing to mask the real meaning.

Cousin Theory: The masses know the rules while the powerful know the exceptions.

Reactions to the COUSIN Theory

One professor was presented with the summary of the COUSIN Theory and agreed that it was very obvious and a fairly good representation of the world of business and how it worked. Another professor was about the presentation. He suggested the COUSIN theory was a cynical view of the world and would result in the institutionalization of people's worst behavior. He said that the "Reality" is a negative depiction and that if the masses know and pursue the reality as the way to success then society is in trouble.

He further commented that there are organizational leaders that are good people and that the rules of orthodoxy are aspirational for good reason. He concluded by saying: "We don't want to teach them the violation of basic morality"

This raised the fundamental question about ethics and morality. Is it right because Me (I), We (family, friends or fraternity), or Thee (scripture, sage or science) determine that it is? There are many groups that would present their own judgment concerning what is right or wrong as there are many absolute authorities. Is transparently exposing an observed behavior threatening to society? Is penetrating the veil of secrecy concerning the practices of some movers and shakers wrong?

The Me, We or Thee Question

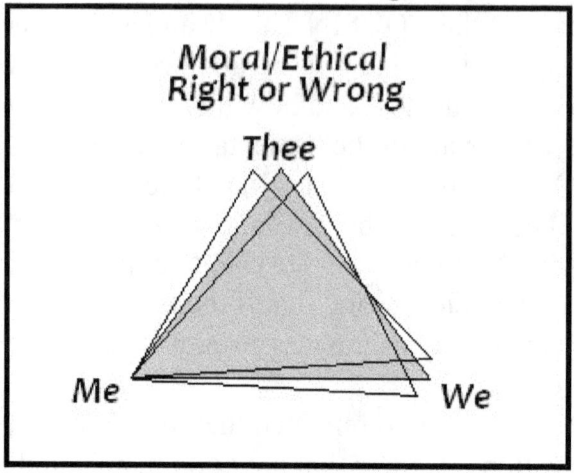

Terms:

CONTROL THE MESSAGE: The first principle of the Cousin Theory, every executive who aspires to be successful must strive for total control over communications about their efforts and enterprise. This will require the suppression of dissenting or contradictory messages.

COUSIN THEORY: The masses know the rules while the creative know the exceptions. The rules are taught and reaffirmed to the rank and file, while the movers and shakers are given exemption. When someone from the masses breaks the rules, through intimidation, negative rewards, or punished they are brought back into compliance.

INFLUENCE THE INFLUENTIAL: The fifth principle of the Cousin Theory, those who are most effective in business are able to get other people to do their bidding. The control of other people results from many actions, but basically understanding what motivates others and use that knowledge.

INTIMIDATION: Making someone submissive through fear and domination.

ME, WE, or THEE Question: Is it right because I (me), We (a group), or Thee (science, sage, seer or scripture) determine that it is?

MOVERS AND SHAKERS, THE: The top 5 percent of the population make things happen. They are often called the movers and shakers. They may or may not be the most creative or wealthiest, but they are the ones who set direction for society and control the money.

NO DISCLOSURE/TRANSPARENCY: The sixth principle of the Cousin Theory, secrecy is the key to success. Consequently, the rules for financial and other disclosures can be manipulated to hide what is truly the important.

OWN THE MARKET: The second principle of the Cousin Theory, successful executives will work to dominate and control the market so their products and services will have the freedom to influence demand and set prices.

SHIFT THE RISK: The fourth principle of the Cousin Theory, a company must limit risk wherever possible. They must assess risk and avoid it or the most effective way is to position the company so that when negative financial consequences result, others will assume responsibility.

UNREGULATED IS BEST: The third principle of the Cousin Theory, the best case for an executive is for their enterprise to operate outside of oversight from governmental regulators, rating agencies, independent auditors, or media watchdogs.